LOVING FAIRFIELD

Joe Pascoe

LOVING FAIRFIELD

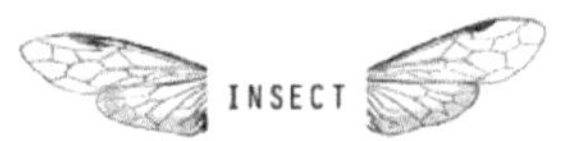

Acknowledgements

Special thanks to the fine shopkeepers, shoppers
and happy children of Station Street, Fairfield, Melbourne.
Always my love to Lyndel Wischer, Eve Pascoe and John
Pascoe
as well as Chuchi, who sniffs out the real scene.
Curatorial Research by Zoe Constantinou, Emma
Fayelecaun (Video), Brooke McColl (CATA) and Adam Bos
(NDIS).

Contents

Preface

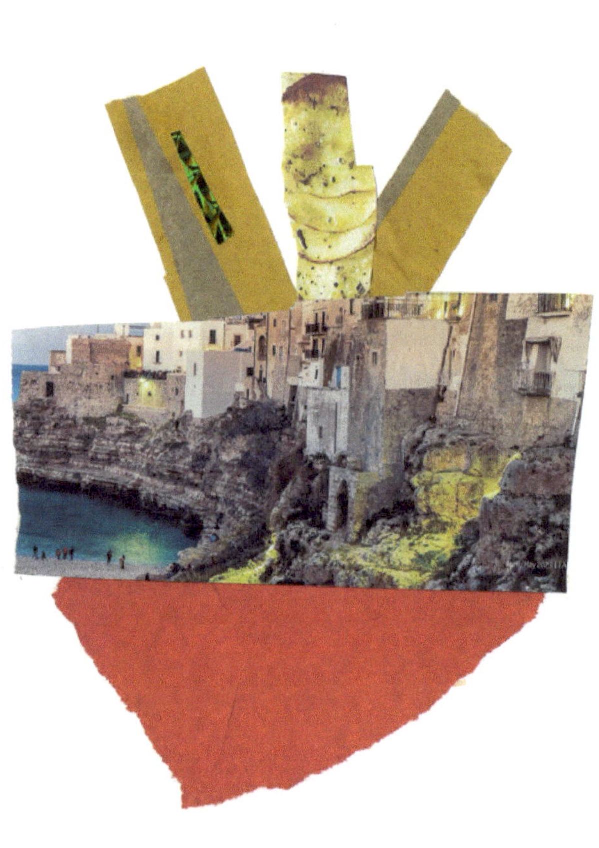

Preface

Fairfield is where diverse peoples have settled, often after long journeys from far away. Its Station Street is something of a welcoming home for many, a casual, happy village.

A charming railway station, a giant wooden dog called Fido and numerous independent shops give it an easy air.

The combination of angle parking and parallel parking let people and cars weave without much honking. A market town in its own style, Fairfield has manners without pretention. You can say hello!

With scissors and coloured papers, along with some poems, I have sought to create an individual idea of the place – like as if Piet Mondrian had visited. Look around and you too will see patterns and shapes behind the more obvious ones of shop goods and people's clothes, under an Australian sky.

Joe Pascoe

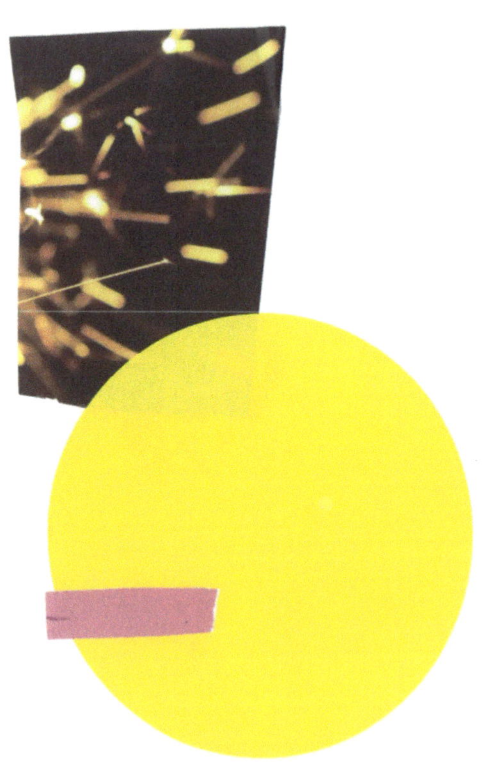

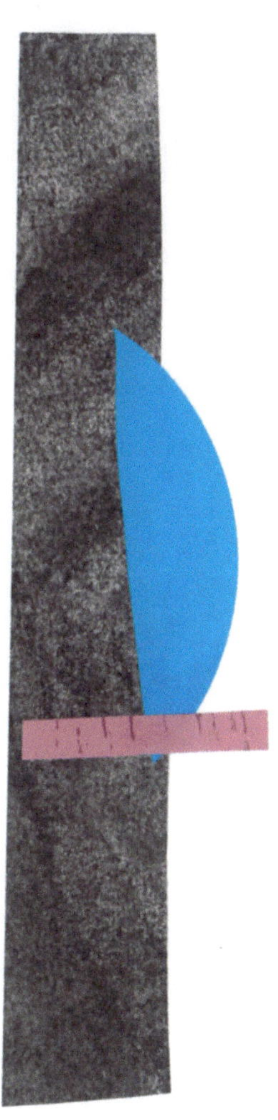

Dogachino

Dog latte
Dogachino
We look after our pets in Ivanhoe
... and Fairfield

Chains tinkle
Owners yawn
It's early here today

Soft paws
No hard claws
Cars go by

We love our pooches
No silly douches
Every dog a sparkle in the eye

Tails twitch
Ears forward and backward
Count the legs, always four

Some are old
Some pups
All friends to all

It's our community
City folk feeling fine
Never still, offering a thrill
Chuchi is mine!

Station Street

Coffee scroll, coffee
Waiting a moment
Cosy in the street
Happily at a table

Chuchi rustling around
Nose left and right
Soft ears back
Bum to me
Now gone off for a sniff

Light foot traffic goes by
Truck idles at the lights
Little breeze clears the air
I hear birds declare
'Station Street, free of despair'

Let troubles go
Enjoy this day
Let it play
Don't deepen your thoughts
Keep yourself neat
It's really a nice street.

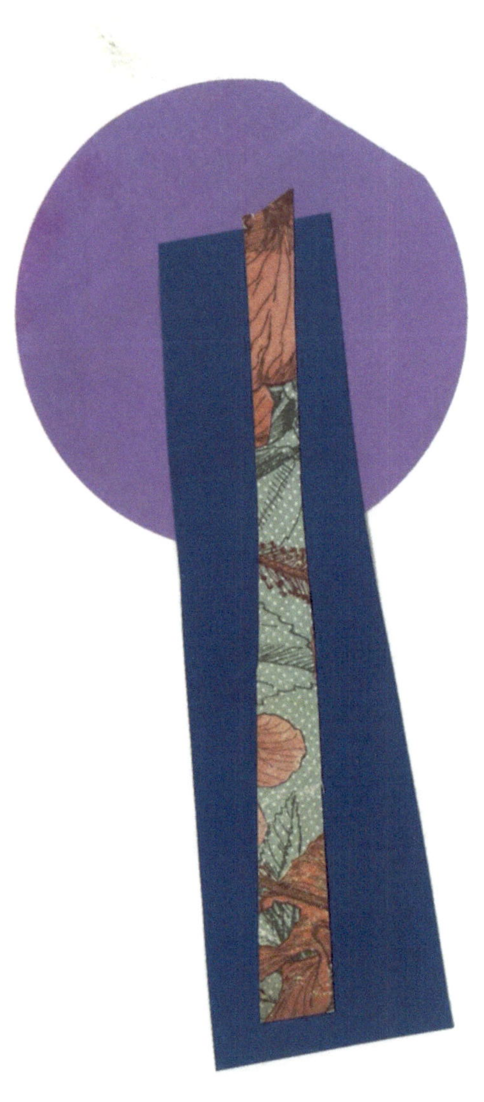

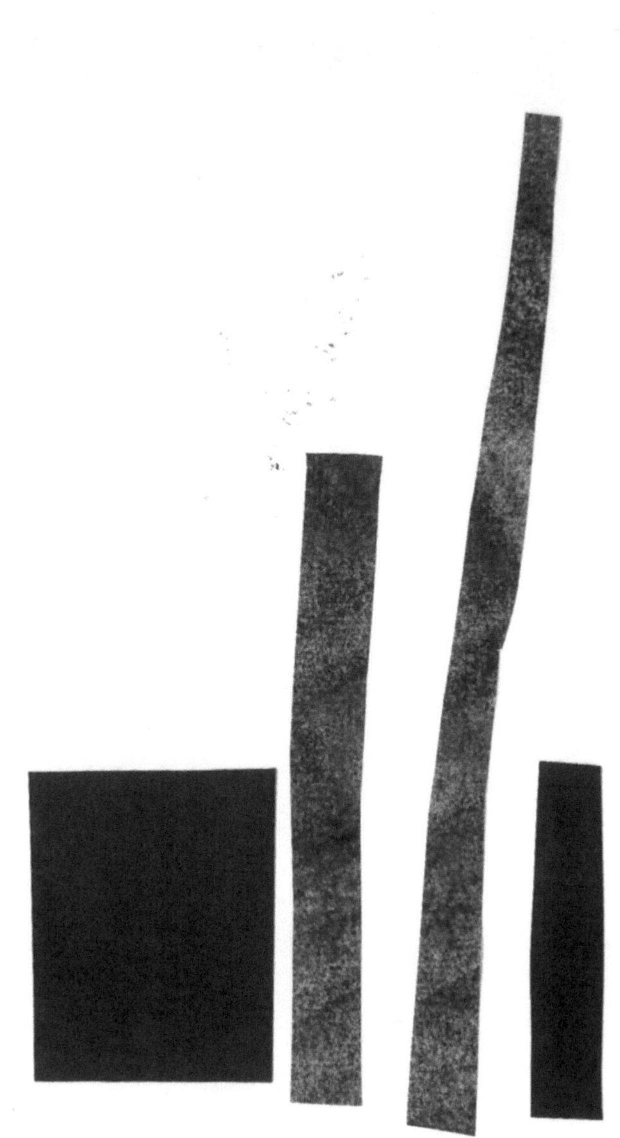

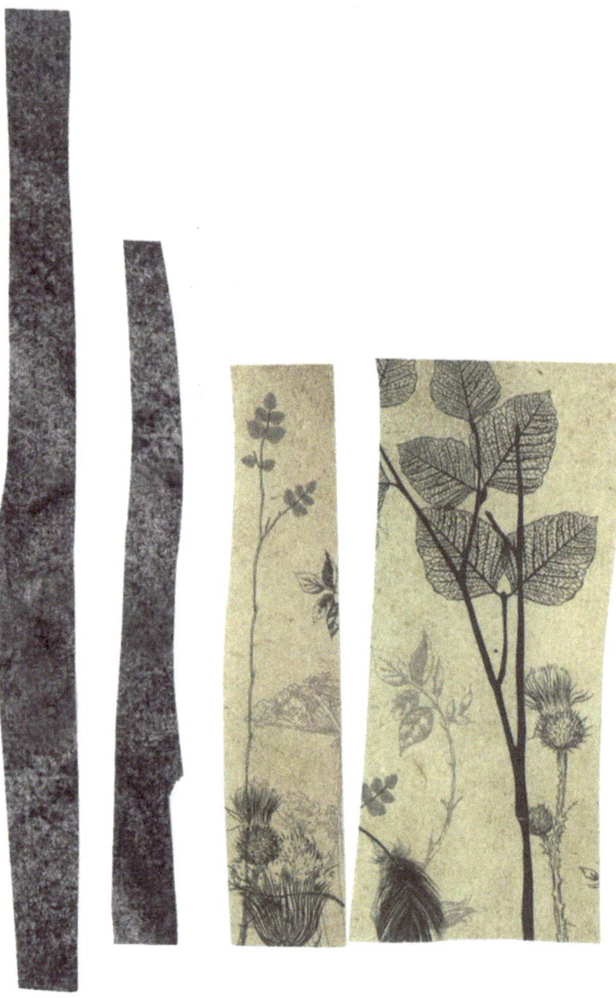

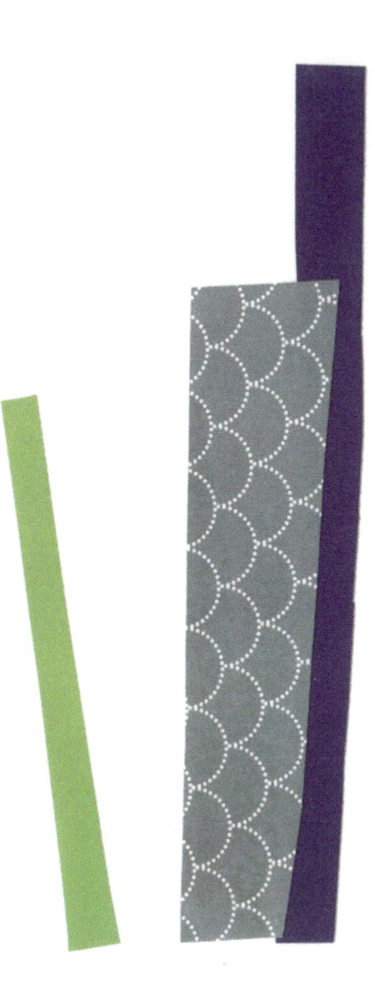
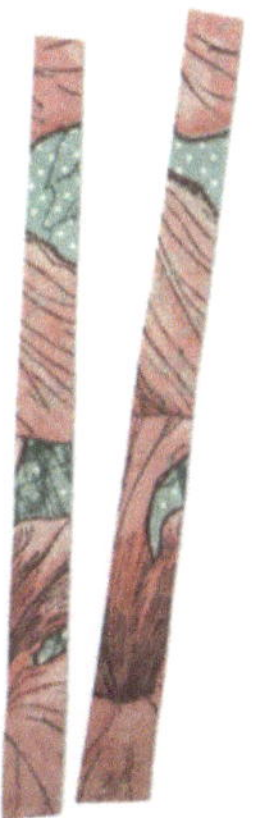

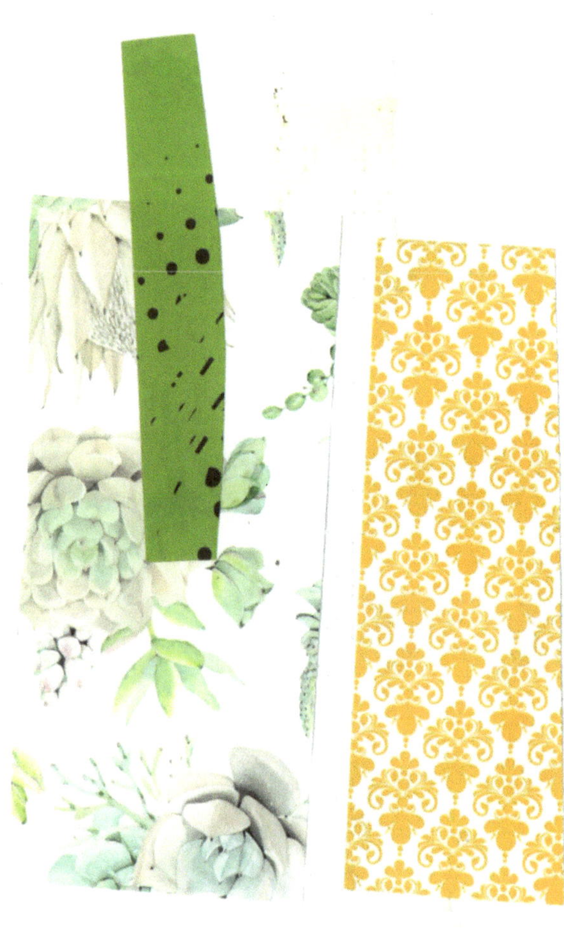

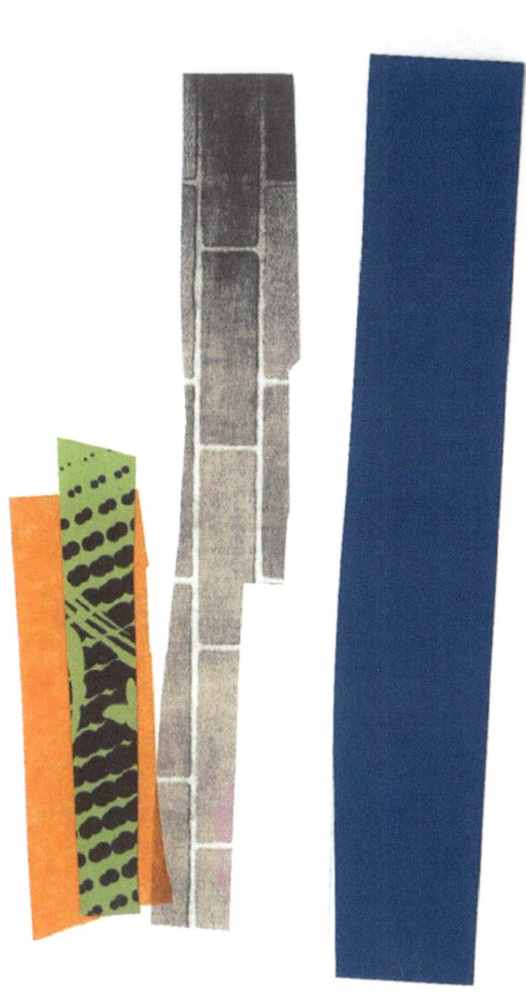

Funny shopping

Went to the bookshop
Next to the pert shop
Near the $2 shop
Felt like a hair cut
Peered through the window
Caped human sculptures being snipped
Stayed out but admired the pantheon of
youth

Lacking patience, thought of something
Not sure what
I'm lazy sometimes
Don't need a book
Or a live rabbit
Possibly a plastic box
Or just keep my hands in pockets
Stretching my legs toward home.

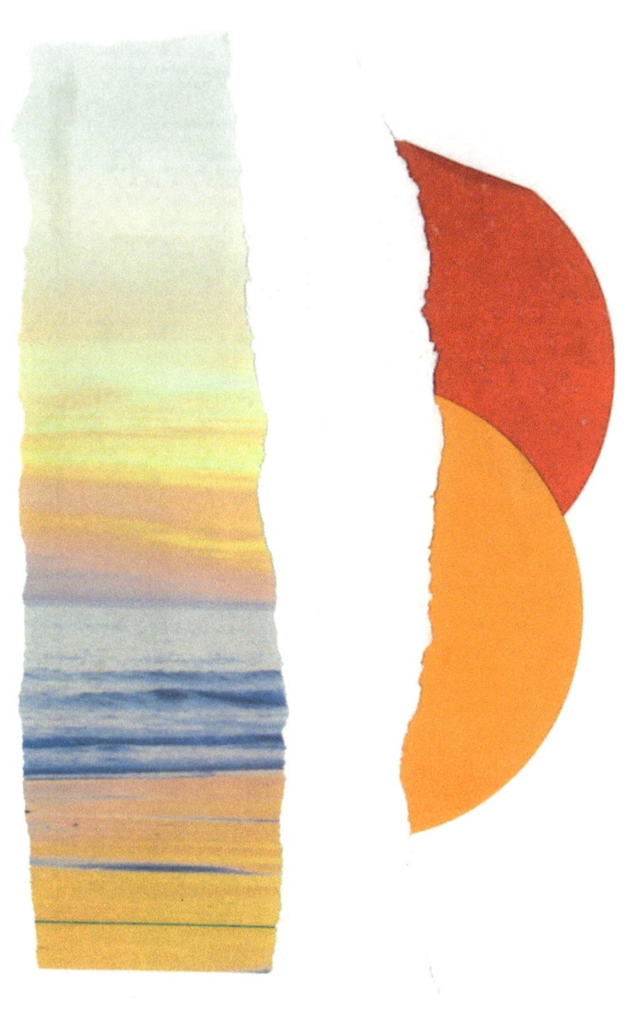

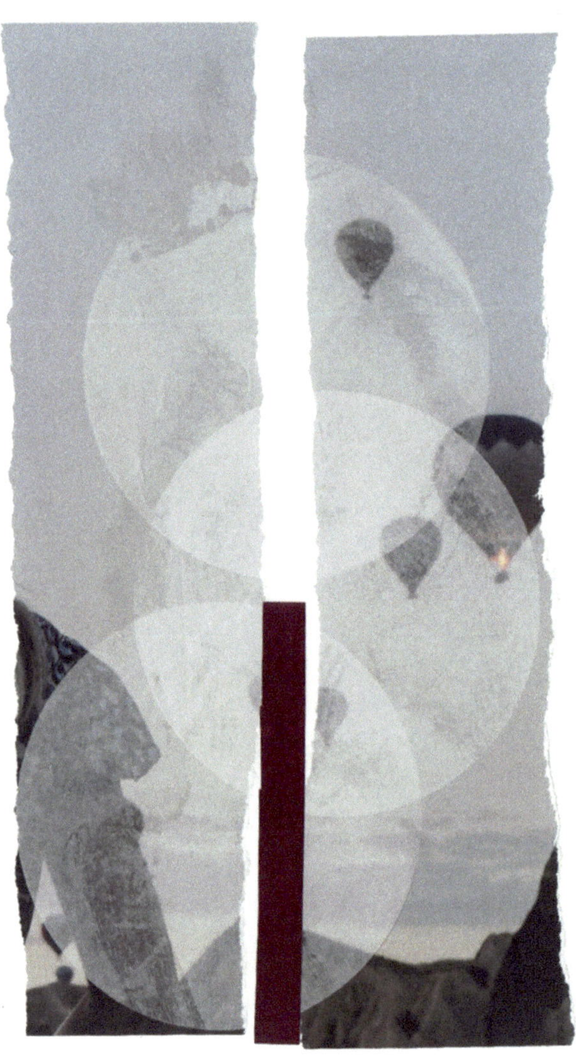

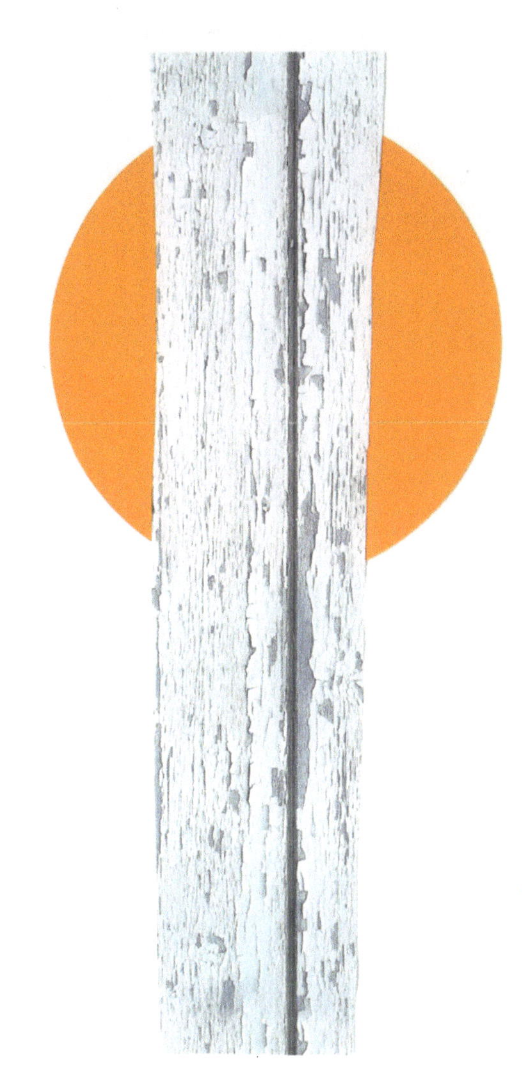

Good times

Sweet baklava
Crunchy pork roll
Easy coffee scroll

Places to eat
Easy to find a seat
On Station Street

Say it once
Say it twice
Toss it up thrice

Fit in well
Go forth and tell
Our little town, no frown.

Buy some stuff
Hand over the dough
Let it grow, kind Station Street.

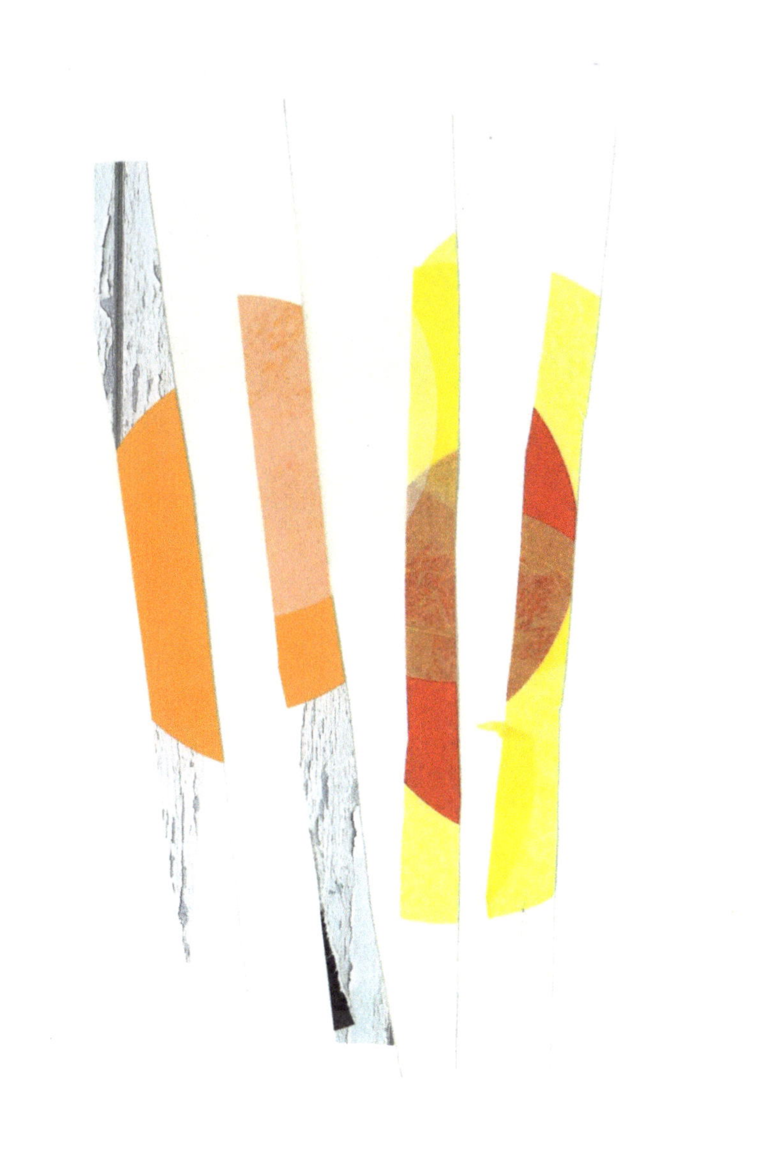

Footpath

Butcher shop laid out
Life sorted for you

Paper shop ready
Great Tattslotto calling out

Tasty souvlaki
Dreaming of yum

Coffee shop beckons
Lips pucker

Shoe shop quiet
Not for me today

Cut flowers brush my jacket
I judge the fruit kindly

Cakes
I already know their worth

Soft footpath rolls on
Kind steps take me along.

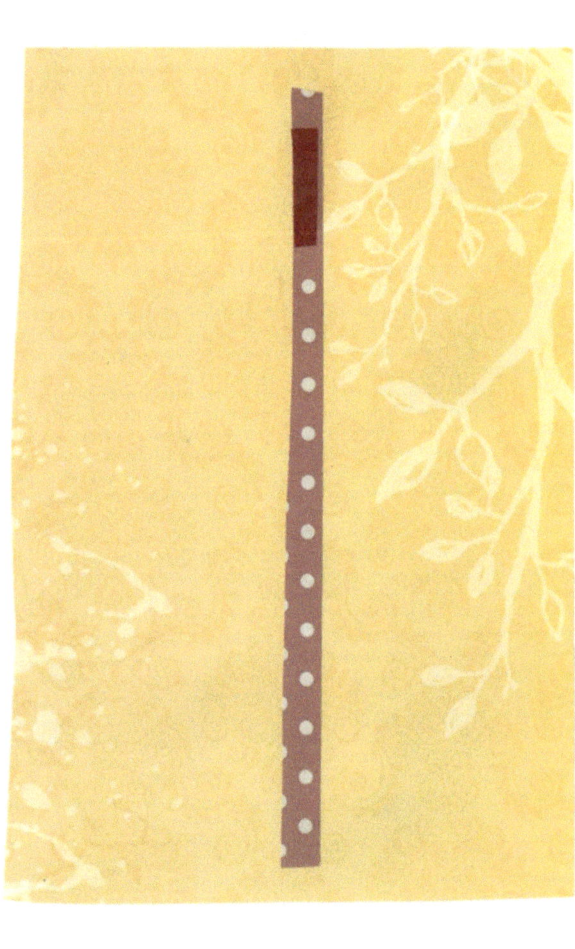

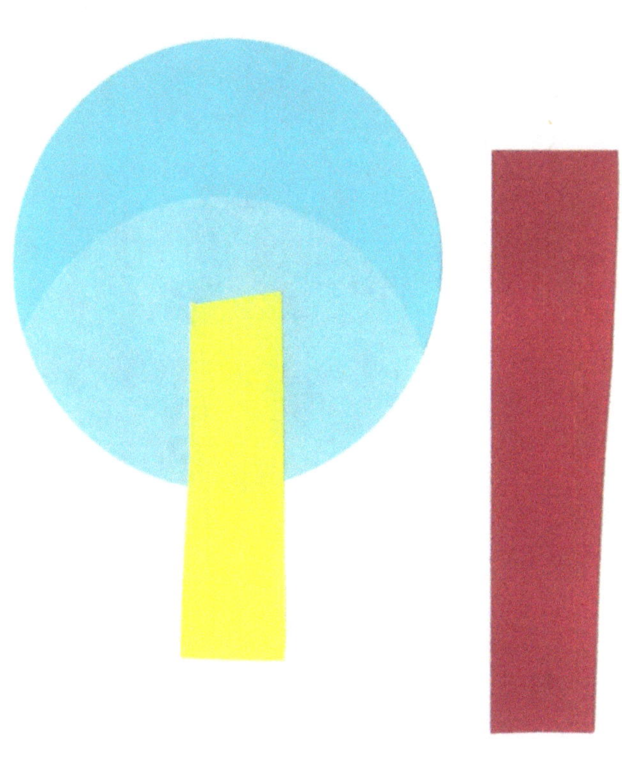

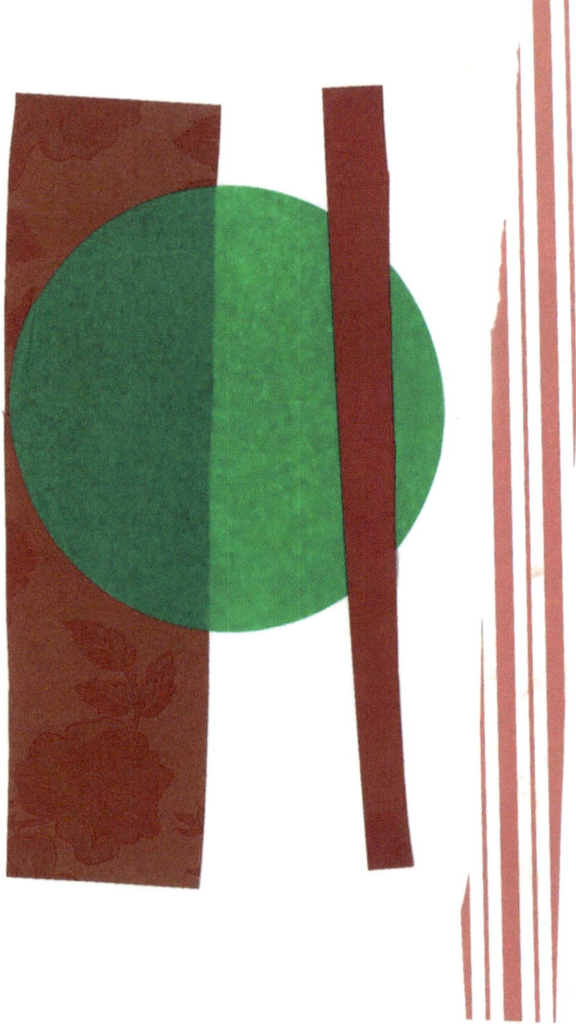

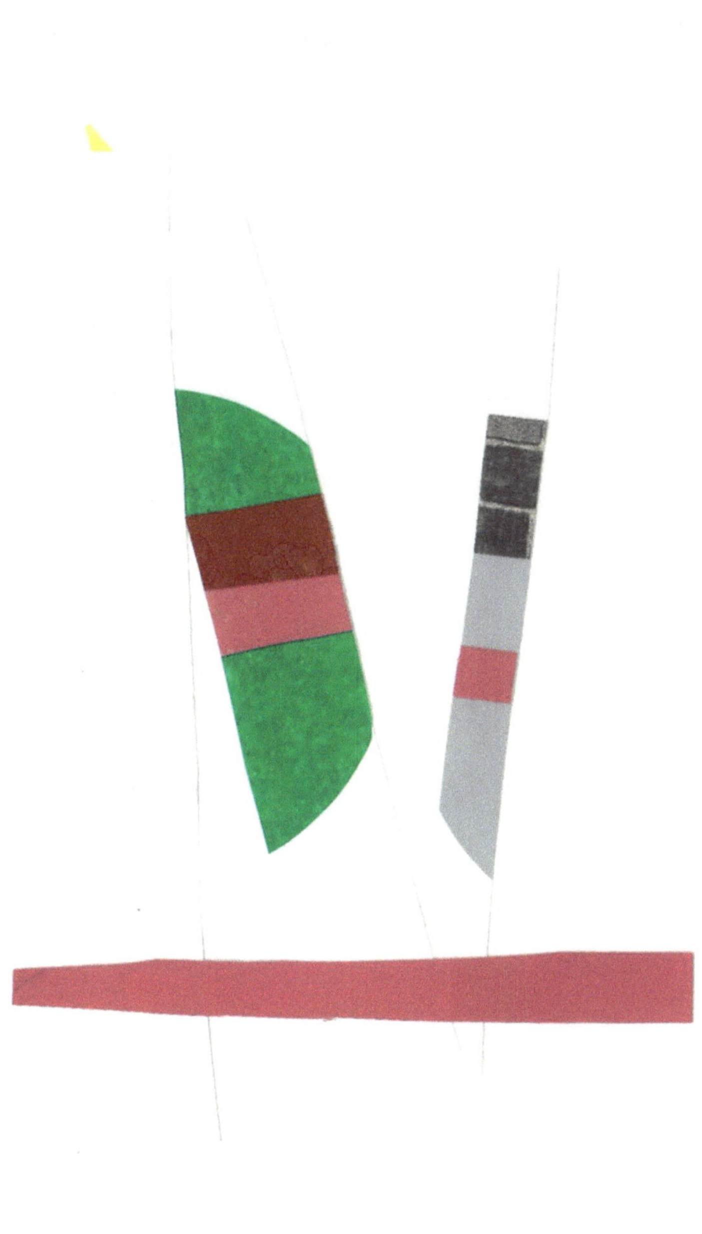

Crocodile smile

Busker on the street
Questions on my mind
How did you get there?
Where do you sleep?

Do they see me?
See me not looking
Does it really matter?
If by you I do creep

Oh busker on the street
Sometimes you do not play
Is that because of a lack of pay?
Or because you cannot find a song to fit this
day?

You look like you have travelled
Practical and worn
Usually you have friends
Throwing words to each other
Some mystery at play

Busker on the street
You are welcome for a while
But don't be a crocodile
No fancy tricks
Just please sing us a song
Help us too, to walk along with a smile.

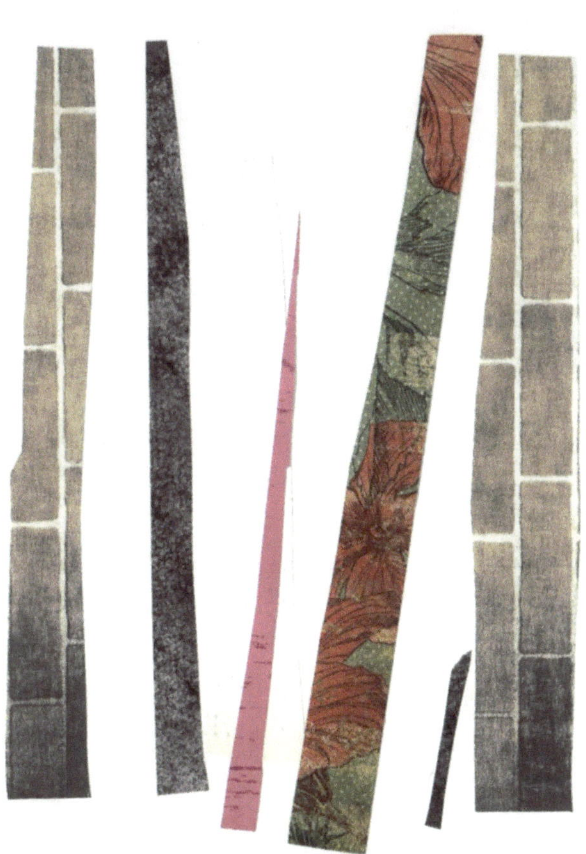

Railway

for Miwa and Marcus

Level crossing dings
Makes me think of Santa
And the gifts he brings

I guess they could vary the tune
But I quite like it
Clattering like a shiny spoon

Formalities over
Wooden chop sticks rise
Always something of a surprise

Cross the steel rails
Admire the engineering
Beautiful train set nearing

Great big things
Little tiny rivets
Metal, wood and rubber
Looking each way
Left, right and straight away
Time to play.

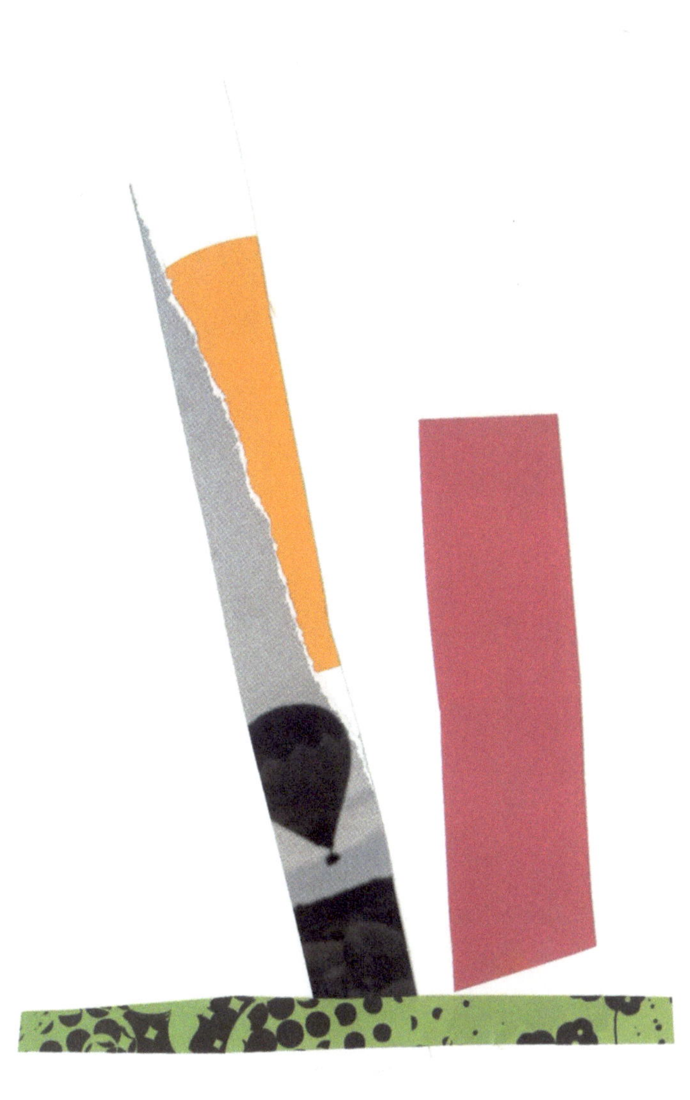

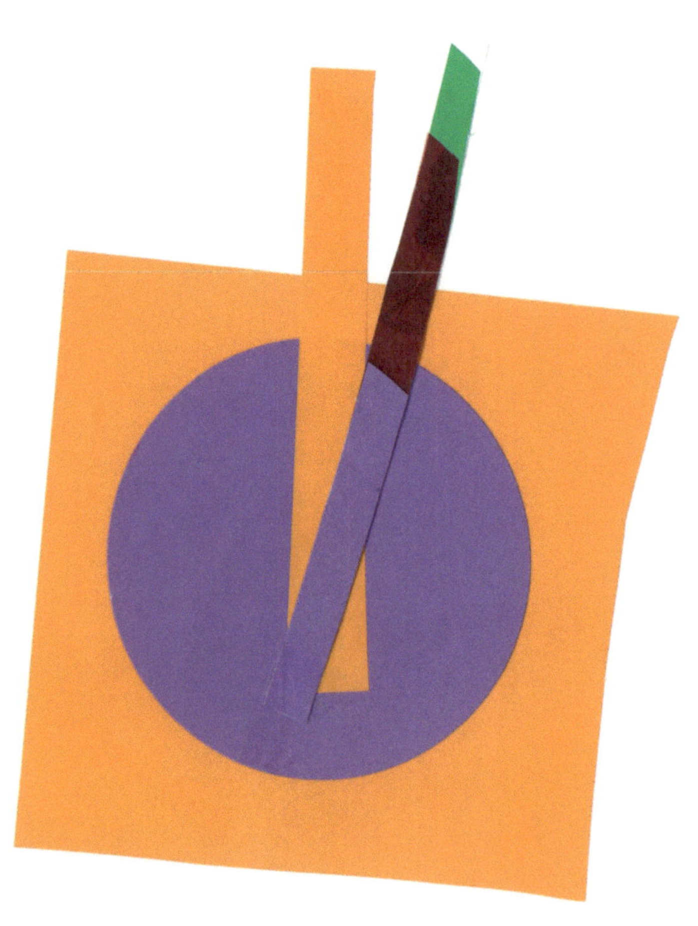

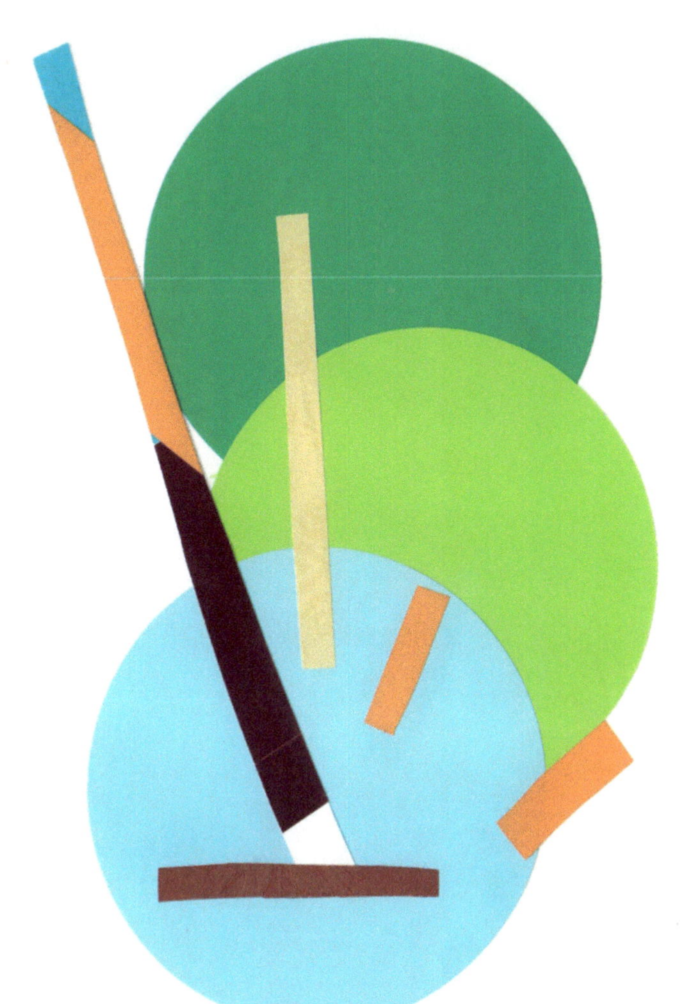